"Love" The Heart of The Bible

Michael Nowlin Jr.

DEDICATION

To those who don't feel loved,

In the sacred words of the Bible, we find the reassurance of a love that surpasses all understanding, a love that knows no boundaries, and a love that is unwavering. When the world's embrace feels distant, when the storms of life leave you feeling alone, remember that you are cherished by the One who created you in His image.

In the book of Psalms, we read, "The Lord is near to the brokenhearted and saves the crushed in spirit" (Psalm 34:18). In your moments of despair, in the depths of your sorrow, He is with you, offering His loving embrace to mend your wounded heart.

You are not defined by the love you receive from others; you are defined by the love of your Creator. In the book of Jeremiah, God declares, "I have loved you with an everlasting love; therefore, I have continued my faithfulness to you" (Jeremiah 31:3). His love is eternal, and His faithfulness knows no end.

When you feel unloved, turn to the words of Jesus, who reminds us, "Come to me, all who labor and are heavy laden, and I will give you rest" (Matthew 11:28). His invitation is open to all, and His love brings peace and solace to the weary heart.

Even in your darkest hours, know that God's love is your guiding star, leading you out of the shadows and into the light. In the book of Romans, we find the words, "For I am sure that neither death nor life, nor angels nor rulers, nor things present nor things to come, nor powers, nor height nor depth, nor anything else in all creation, will be able to separate us from the love of God in Christ Jesus our Lord" (Romans 8:38-39). His love is unshakable and will never let you go.

To those who don't feel loved, remember that God's love is a constant presence in your life, a refuge in times of trouble, and a promise of eternal love that is yours to embrace. In Him, you are deeply and unconditionally loved.

With faith and love,

Bishop Michael Nowlin Jr.

Acknowledgements:

I would like to express my sincere gratitude to Nowlin Publishing for their unwavering support and belief in this project. Your dedication to excellence and commitment to bringing meaningful content to the world has been instrumental in shaping this book.

I am also deeply thankful to ABL Ministries for their encouragement and inspiration throughout the writing process. Your ministry's passion for spreading hope and light has been a guiding force behind the themes explored in these pages.

Additionally, I extend my heartfelt appreciation to CBDCF for their invaluable contributions to the research and development of this book. Your commitment to making a positive impact in communities worldwide has been truly inspiring.

Special thanks to ABL Publishing for their collaboration and assistance in bringing this book to fruition. Your expertise and professionalism have been indispensable in ensuring the quality and success of this project.

Finally, I am grateful to all the readers and supporters who have embraced this journey with open hearts. Your enthusiasm and encouragement have fueled my passion for sharing the message of hope with the world.

Together, may we continue to discover the harmony of hope in every aspect of our lives.

Warm regards,

Michael Nowlin Jr

Title: "Love: The Heart of the Bible"

Introduction:

This intro to the "Heart of the Bible" beautifully sets the stage for a profound journey through the pages of the Bible, inviting readers to embark on an exploration of the multifaceted concept of love. This introduction highlights the centrality of divine love in the sacred text, emphasizing that love is not just a theme but the very heart of the Bible.

As we journey through the Old Testament and the New Testament, we are promised an in-depth exploration of the various dimensions of divine love. Through stories, verses, and teachings, readers are invited to uncover the depth, breadth, and transformative power of love as portrayed in the Bible. This journey promises to be both enlightening and spiritually enriching, providing insights into the significance of love as a driving force in the biblical narrative.

The introduction serves as an engaging and promising prelude to a deeper dive into the heart of the Bible, where the essence of divine love is waiting to be discovered and embraced. It sets the tone for a meaningful exploration of the Bible's timeless message of love, compassion, and redemption.

Chapter 1
"Love in Creation"

God's love is evident in the act of creation.

The idea that God's love is evident in the act of creation is a significant theological concept in many religious traditions, including Christianity.

Gift of Existence: God's act of creating the world and everything in it can be seen as an expression of divine love. By bringing the universe into being, God grants the gift of existence to all living things. This act of creation is an ultimate demonstration of love because it allows for life to flourish and for individuals to experience the world.

Beauty and Diversity: The diversity and beauty of the natural world are often seen as reflections of God's love. The intricacy and variety of creatures, landscapes, and ecosystems showcase the richness of God's creative love. The existence of diverse life forms and ecosystems allows for wonder and appreciation of God's creative hand.

Provision and Sustenance: God's creation provides for the needs of living beings. The Earth is abundant with resources that sustain life, from food and water to shelter and beauty. This provision is an expression of God's love and care for His creation.

Order and Purpose: The order and purpose in the natural world reflect the intention and love of the Creator. The laws of nature, the cycles of life, and the balance in ecosystems all demonstrate a design that supports life. This order and purpose are seen as a reflection of God's wisdom and love.

Responsibility as Stewards: In many religious traditions, the act of creation comes with a call to stewardship. The responsibility to care for the Earth and its creatures is a way of responding to God's love for His creation. It emphasizes the need to protect and preserve the environment as an act of love and gratitude.

Redemption and Restoration: In some theological perspectives, the act of creation is seen as the beginning of a divine plan that includes redemption and restoration. God's love is evident in His commitment to restoring and renewing His creation, even in the face of human failings and the effects of sin.

Human Dignity: The creation of humanity in the image of God is a profound expression of God's love. This act bestows a unique dignity and value on every individual. It affirms that each person is created with purpose and worth, and this is a powerful reflection of God's love.

The act of creation is often interpreted as a fundamental demonstration of God's love in religious thought. It shows God's intention for life, His provision, His care, and His desire for a loving relationship with His creation. This understanding of creation as an act of love is central to many religious worldviews and serves as a foundation for ethical and moral considerations regarding the treatment of the environment and all living beings.

Humanity being created in the image of God, designed to love and be loved.

The significance of humanity being created in the image of God, designed to love and be loved, is a central theological concept with profound implications for our understanding of human identity, purpose, and relationships. Here are some key reflections on this significance:

Inherent Dignity: Being created in the image of God imbues every individual with inherent dignity and worth. This concept affirms the sanctity of human life, recognizing that every person possesses a unique and irreplaceable value. It forms the foundation of human rights and the belief that every individual should be treated with respect and love.

Capacity for Love: One of the defining characteristics of being created in God's image is the capacity for love. Just as God is love, humans are designed to love and to be loved. This capacity for love extends to love for God, love for others, and even self-love. It underpins the moral imperative to love one another.

Relational Nature: The idea of being created in God's image also emphasizes the relational nature of humanity. Just as God exists in a triune relationship (Father, Son, and Holy Spirit), humans are created to exist in relationships. This includes relationships with God, with other people, and with the world around us. Love is at the heart of these relationships.

Moral Responsibility: The recognition of humanity's divine image carries moral responsibilities. It implies that humans are called to reflect the attributes of God, including love, compassion, justice, and mercy. This responsibility to emulate God's character through love and righteousness guides ethical decision-making.

Purpose and Meaning: Understanding that humans are created in the image of God provides a sense of purpose and meaning to life. It suggests that each person has a unique role to play in fulfilling God's plan and in contributing to the well-being of the world. This purpose often involves acts of love and service.

Empowerment for Positive Change: The belief in being created in God's image can empower individuals to make positive changes in the world. Recognizing that they share in God's creative and loving nature, people are inspired to work toward justice, reconciliation, and the betterment of society.

Redemption and Transformation: When humans recognize their divine image despite their imperfections, it opens the door to redemption and transformation. This means that despite human failings and sins, there is the potential for individuals to experience God's transformative love and be restored to the image of God through faith and repentance.

The belief that humanity is created in the image of God and designed to love and be loved is a fundamental concept that shapes religious and ethical perspectives. It highlights the sacredness of each person, the importance of love and relationships, and the moral responsibility to reflect God's character in our actions. This understanding of human identity provides a rich foundation for moral and ethical frameworks, promoting compassion, justice, and the pursuit of a loving and meaningful life.

Chapter 2
"Covenantal Love"

Covenant in the Bible and how it signifies a loving relationship between God and humanity.

The concept of a covenant in the Bible is a central and profound theme that signifies a loving and faithful relationship between God and humanity. A covenant is more than just a contract; it represents a sacred bond and a promise of mutual commitment.

Definition of Covenant:
- In the Bible, a covenant is a solemn agreement or contract between two parties, often sealed with a ceremony or a sign.
- It goes beyond a mere legal or transactional relationship; it carries the weight of commitment, trust, and loyalty.

God's Initiative:
- Covenants in the Bible are typically initiated by God. They are divine promises and commitments to humanity.
- This emphasizes the idea that God takes the first step in establishing a relationship with His people.

Expressing God's Love:
- Covenants in the Bible are a way for God to express His deep love for humanity. They demonstrate His desire for a close and loving relationship with His people.
- The covenants often involve promises of protection, provision, and guidance, all rooted in God's love and care.

Examples of Covenants:
- The Abrahamic Covenant: In the covenant with Abraham, God promised to make him the father of a great nation and to bless all the nations of the earth through his descendants (Genesis 12:1-3). This covenant signifies God's love and commitment to His people.

- The Mosaic Covenant: The covenant given to Moses on Mount Sinai, including the Ten Commandments, is a covenant that outlines God's expectations for His people. It reflects God's desire for a just and righteous relationship with humanity.
- The New Covenant: The New Testament introduces the concept of the New Covenant, established through Jesus Christ. It signifies God's ultimate

act of love and redemption, as Jesus' sacrifice brings forgiveness and a renewed relationship between God and humanity (Jeremiah 31:31-34).

Reciprocal Commitment:
- While God initiates covenants, they often require a response from humanity. The covenant relationship involves both parties committing to uphold their responsibilities.
- This reciprocal commitment underscores the idea of a loving and mutual relationship between God and His people.

Renewal and Restoration:
- Covenants in the Bible are often renewed, especially in times when the people of God stray from their commitment. This reflects God's enduring love and His desire to restore the relationship with His people.

Signs and Seals:
- Many covenants in the Bible are accompanied by signs or seals that serve as a reminder of the covenant. For example, the rainbow is a sign of God's covenant with Noah (Genesis 9:13), and circumcision was a sign of the covenant with Abraham (Genesis 17:11).

The concept of covenant in the Bible is a testament to God's love and faithfulness to humanity. It signifies a loving and committed relationship in which God takes the initiative to establish and maintain a bond with His people. The covenants in the Bible are not merely legal agreements; they are expressions of divine love, grace, and the desire for a close and enduring relationship with humanity.

Stories like the covenant with Noah and the Israelites.

The stories of the covenants with Noah and the Israelites in the Bible offer valuable lessons about God's loving relationship with humanity and the significance of these covenants:

.

Covenant with Noah:
The covenant with Noah, found in Genesis 9:8-17, teaches us the following: God's Mercy and Renewal: After the Great Flood, God made a covenant with Noah and all living creatures, promising never to destroy the earth with a flood again. This covenant demonstrates God's mercy and His commitment to giving humanity a fresh start. It teaches us that even in times of great crisis and cleansing, God's love and mercy prevail.

Symbolic Significance: The rainbow serves as a sign of this covenant. It reminds us that God keeps His promises. When we see a rainbow, it's a reminder of God's faithfulness and love.

Stewardship of Creation: The covenant with Noah also emphasizes humanity's responsibility as stewards of the earth and its creatures. We are entrusted with the care of God's creation. This teaches us the importance of environmental responsibility and ethical treatment of all living beings.

Covenant with the Israelites (Sinai Covenant):
The covenant made with the Israelites at Mount Sinai, including the giving of the Ten Commandments, found in Exodus 19-24, offers important lessons:

God's Expectations: The covenant at Sinai outlined God's expectations for His people. The Ten Commandments and other laws provided a moral and ethical framework for the Israelites. This teaches us that a loving relationship with God includes living in accordance with His values and principles.

Responsibility and Accountability: The covenant with the Israelites introduced the idea of responsibility and accountability. God's people were expected to obey His commands, and they would be held accountable for their actions. This emphasizes that love and obedience go hand in hand in a covenant relationship.

Community and Mutual Commitment: The Israelite covenant was communal, and the people collectively accepted the covenant's terms. This illustrates the idea of a collective and mutual commitment to God. It teaches us that a loving relationship with God is not just an individual endeavor but involves a community of believers.

Repentance and Renewal: Throughout the history of the Israelites, we see instances of breaking the covenant and God's subsequent forgiveness and renewal of the covenant. This demonstrates God's willingness to forgive and restore the covenant relationship when people repent. It teaches us the importance of repentance and God's enduring love.

Both of these covenants emphasize God's love, mercy, and commitment to humanity. They show that even when we falter or face challenges, God's love remains steadfast. These stories teach us about the nature of a loving covenant relationship with God, characterized by faith, obedience, accountability, and the potential for renewal and restoration.

Chapter 3
"Unconditional Love"

God's unconditional love as demonstrated in the parable of the Prodigal Son and through God's grace and forgiveness.

The theme of God's unconditional love as demonstrated in the parable of the Prodigal Son and through God's grace and forgiveness is a profound and heartwarming aspect of Christian theology.

Parable of the Prodigal Son:
The Parable of the Prodigal Son is found in the New Testament in the Gospel of Luke, specifically in Luke 15:11-32. This parable tells the story of a wayward son who squanders his inheritance in a far-off country and ends up in dire circumstances. However, upon his return home, his father not only forgives him but also celebrates his return with great joy. Here are key aspects of God's unconditional love demonstrated in this parable:

Unconditional Forgiveness: The father's immediate forgiveness of the prodigal son represents God's boundless capacity for forgiveness. Despite the son's rebellion and poor choices, the father is quick to extend love and acceptance, exemplifying the idea that God's love is not dependent on our merits.

Restoration and Redemption: The father's embrace of the prodigal son symbolizes God's desire for the restoration and redemption of wayward souls. This demonstrates that God's love seeks not only to forgive but also to bring individuals back into a loving relationship.

Joyful Reconciliation: The parable underscores the joy that God experiences when a lost soul repents and returns. The celebration of the prodigal son's return signifies the immense joy in heaven when a sinner repents (Luke 15:7). This speaks to the depth of God's love for each individual.

Equality of Love: The parable also addresses the elder brother's reaction to his younger brother's return. The father's response emphasizes that God's love is equally extended to all, regardless of past actions. Both sons are loved, and God's love knows no partiality.

God's Grace and Forgiveness:
The theme of God's unconditional love, grace, and forgiveness is not limited to this parable but is woven throughout the Christian message. It teaches several important lessons:

Infinite Patience: God's love is patient and enduring. It waits for the wayward to return and embraces them with open arms.

Complete Forgiveness: God's forgiveness is complete and absolute. When we turn to God with a repentant heart, our sins are forgiven, and we are made new.

No Earning Required: God's love and grace cannot be earned; they are freely given. This concept underscores that we don't have to be perfect to experience God's love and forgiveness.

Transformation and Growth: God's love and forgiveness are transformative. They enable us to grow and change, just as the prodigal son experienced a change of heart.

Unfailing Love: God's love never wavers or diminishes, regardless of our actions. It is steadfast and eternal.

The theme of God's unconditional love as portrayed in the Parable of the Prodigal Son and throughout Christian theology emphasizes the depth of divine love, grace, and forgiveness. It assures us that, no matter how far we may have strayed, God's love is always available for those who seek reconciliation and a loving relationship with the Creator.

God's love is not based on our merit but on His nature.

The concept that God's love is not based on our merit but on His nature is a fundamental and comforting aspect of many religious and spiritual traditions. It has profound implications for our understanding of divine love, human worthiness, and the nature of God. Here are some reflections on this idea:

Unconditional Love: The idea that God's love is not contingent on our merit means that it is unconditional. God's love is not earned through good deeds or lost through mistakes; it is constant and unwavering. This provides a profound sense of security and reassurance for believers, knowing that they are loved in their entirety, flaws and all.

Infinite Grace: God's love is often associated with His infinite grace. Grace is the unmerited favor of God, given freely to humanity. It is not something that can be worked for or deserved. This concept highlights the generosity and boundless nature of God's love.

Equality of Love: The understanding that God's love is not earned means that it is extended equally to all. It doesn't matter one's past, social status, or deeds; God's love is available to every individual. This promotes inclusivity and breaks down barriers that might otherwise hinder people from seeking a relationship with the divine.

Relief from Perfectionism: Belief in God's love not based on merit can provide relief from the burden of perfectionism. It encourages individuals to embrace their imperfections and acknowledge their need for divine love and grace. This can lead to greater self-acceptance and a healthier self-image.

Encouragement for Change: Paradoxically, the knowledge that God's love is not based on our merit can encourage personal growth and transformation. When we realize that we are loved as we are, it can inspire us to change for the better, driven by gratitude for God's love.

Deeper Understanding of God: Recognizing that God's love is intrinsic to His nature leads to a deeper understanding of God's character. It emphasizes God's benevolence, compassion, and desire for a loving relationship with humanity.

Moral and Ethical Implications: This concept encourages ethical behavior not to earn God's love but as a response to it. Believers are motivated to act in ways that reflect God's love and grace, promoting kindness, mercy, and justice.

The idea that God's love is not based on our merit but on His nature is a foundational and comforting belief in many religious faiths. It fosters a sense of security, inclusivity, and a deeper understanding of the divine. It reminds us that God's love is boundless and freely given, offering hope and encouragement to all who seek a loving and transformative relationship with the Creator.

Chapter 4
"Love for One Another"

The New Testament's emphasis on love for one another, as taught by Jesus.

The New Testament places a significant emphasis on love for one another, as taught by Jesus. This theme is central to Jesus' teachings and is found throughout the writings of the apostles and early Christian communities.

The Great Commandment: In the New Testament, Jesus emphasizes the greatest commandment, which is to love God with all one's heart, soul, and mind and to love one's neighbor as oneself (Matthew 22:37-40). This two-fold command encapsulates the essence of Christian love and guides believers in their relationships with both God and fellow humans.

The New Commandment: Jesus introduced a "new commandment" to His disciples, instructing them to love one another as He loved them (John 13:34). This love is characterized by selflessness, sacrificial action, and genuine care for others. It sets a high standard for Christian love.

The Parable of the Good Samaritan: In the Parable of the Good Samaritan (Luke 10:25-37), Jesus teaches the importance of showing love and compassion to those in need, even to those who may be considered outsiders or enemies. This parable challenges the boundaries of love and neighborliness.

Forgiveness: Jesus emphasizes forgiveness as an integral aspect of love. He instructs His followers to forgive those who wrong them and to seek reconciliation (Matthew 6:14-15). This highlights the restorative nature of love.

Love for Enemies: Jesus teaches that love should extend even to one's enemies. In the Sermon on the Mount, He instructs His disciples to love and pray for those who persecuted them (Matthew 5:43-48). This radical form of love challenges conventional notions of love and expands its scope.

The Parable of the Sheep and Goats: In the Parable of the Sheep and Goats (Matthew 25:31-46), Jesus underscores the importance of showing love and care for the marginalized, the hungry, the sick, and those in need.

He identifies acts of love and service to these individuals as acts of love toward Him.

Love in the Early Church: The apostles, who were taught by Jesus, carried His message of love forward in the early Christian community. Their writings, found in the New Testament epistles, emphasize the importance of love, unity, and caring for one another within the Christian community.

Love as the Mark of Discipleship: In the Gospel of John, Jesus states that love for one another will be the distinguishing mark of His disciples (John 13:35). This love serves as a testimony to the world of their identity as followers of Christ.

Fruit of the Spirit: The apostle Paul, in his letter to the Galatians, describes love as one of the fruits of the Spirit (Galatians 5:22). This signifies that love is a result of a life led by the Holy Spirit and is essential for Christian living.

The New Testament's emphasis on love for one another, as taught by Jesus, underscores the foundational role of love in Christian faith and practice. It is a love that extends beyond sentiment and encompasses actions, relationships, and attitudes. This love reflects the divine love of God and serves as a testimony to the transformative power of Christ's teachings in the lives of believers and in the broader community.

The "Golden Rule" and the commandment to love your neighbor as yourself.

The "Golden Rule" and the commandment to love your neighbor as yourself are two foundational ethical teachings found in the New Testament, both of which are closely associated with the teachings of Jesus. These principles emphasize the importance of love, compassion, and moral conduct in the Christian life. Here's an investigation of each concept:

The Golden Rule:

- The "Golden Rule" is expressed in various forms across different cultures and religious traditions, but it is most famously associated with Jesus' teaching. In the Gospel of Matthew, Jesus articulates the Golden Rule as follows: "So whatever you wish that others would do to you, do also to them, for this is the Law and the Prophets" (Matthew 7:12).
- This principle encourages empathy and compassion. It instructs individuals to treat others with the same kindness, fairness, and respect that

they themselves desire. In essence, it's a call to ethical reciprocity.

- The Golden Rule is not limited to Christian ethics; it has universal applicability and resonates with many moral and philosophical systems. It promotes a sense of fairness, empathy, and the consideration of the well-being of others.

The Commandment to Love Your Neighbor as Yourself:

- The commandment to love your neighbor as yourself is deeply rooted in the Old Testament, specifically in Leviticus 19:18: "You shall not take vengeance or bear a grudge against the sons of your own people, but you shall love your neighbor as yourself: I am the Lord."
- Jesus reaffirmed and elevated this commandment. In the New Testament, He declared it one of the two greatest commandments, alongside the commandment to love God with all one's heart (Matthew 22:37-40).
- Loving your neighbor as yourself extends the principle of love to include not only how we treat others but how we perceive their needs and well-being. It calls for selflessness and genuine concern for the welfare of those around us.
- The parable of the Good Samaritan, mentioned earlier, is a powerful illustration of this commandment. It emphasizes the idea that our neighbor is anyone in need, regardless of their background or circumstances.

Both the Golden Rule and the commandment to love your neighbor as yourself are foundational to Christian ethics and provide guidance for moral conduct. They emphasize the importance of empathy, selflessness, and the active expression of love in one's interactions with others. These teachings promote the idea that a life of faith is reflected not only in one's relationship with God but also in one's relationship with fellow human beings, embodying principles of compassion, justice, and kindness.

Chapter 5
"Agape Love"

Agape love, selfless and sacrificial love.

Agape love, often referred to as selfless and sacrificial love, is a profound and transcendent concept found in various religious and philosophical traditions. It goes beyond romantic love (eros) and familial love (storge) and is often considered the highest form of love. Here's a deeper dive into the concept of agape love:

The Origin of Agape Love:

- The term "agape" has its roots in ancient Greek, and it was used to describe a unique and selfless form of love.
- In Christian theology, agape love is closely associated with the teachings of Jesus Christ and the New Testament. It is considered the purest form of love, reflecting God's divine love for humanity and the sacrificial love of Jesus in His crucifixion.

Selfless and Sacrificial Nature:

- Agape love is characterized by its selfless and sacrificial nature. It is a love that gives without expecting anything in return.
- It involves acts of kindness, compassion, and care for others, often at personal cost or inconvenience. Agape love seeks the well-being and welfare of others.

Universal and Unconditional:

- Agape love is not limited to one's family, friends, or those who share a common bond. It extends to all people, including strangers and even those considered adversaries or enemies.
- It is unconditional, meaning it does not depend on the recipient's worthiness or the expectation of reciprocity.

Action-Oriented Love:

- Agape love is not merely a feeling or sentiment; it is primarily an action-oriented love. It is demonstrated through deeds and behaviors that show care, empathy, and compassion.
- It involves putting the needs and well-being of others ahead of one's own desires and interests.

Motivated by Faith and Virtue:
- In Christian contexts, agape love is often seen as a response to God's love and grace. It is rooted in faith and a desire to reflect the love of God in one's life.
- It aligns with virtues such as patience, kindness, humility, and forgiveness, as outlined in the biblical passage known as "the Love Chapter" in 1 Corinthians 13.

Transformational Power:
- Agape love has the power to transform individuals and relationships. It can heal divisions, foster reconciliation, and promote unity among diverse groups.
- It challenges self-centeredness and encourages individuals to rise above their own desires to serve and love others selflessly.

Universal Applicability:
- While agape love has strong roots in Christian theology, its principles of selflessness and sacrificial love have universal applicability. They resonate with people of various faiths and philosophical backgrounds.
- Agape love is often seen as a guiding principle for building a more compassionate and just society.

Agape love represents the highest form of love, characterized by selflessness, sacrifice, and a deep commitment to the well-being of others. It is a concept that transcends religious and cultural boundaries, inspiring individuals to love unconditionally and act with kindness and compassion toward all. This type of love is considered not only a virtue but a transformative force that can bring about positive change in individuals and society as a whole.

1 Corinthians 13, often referred to as the "Love Chapter".

1 Corinthians 13, often referred to as the "Love Chapter," is a profound and poetic passage from the New Testament that offers timeless lessons about the nature of love. It provides a blueprint for how love should be expressed and experienced. Here are some key teachings that can be gleaned from this chapter:

Love is Essential: The opening verses of 1 Corinthians 13 stress the indispensability of love. It underscores that without love, even the most extraordinary gifts and actions are meaningless. Love is the foundation of all Christian virtues and should be at the center of our lives.

Characteristics of Love: The chapter outlines specific characteristics of love, which include patience, kindness, humility, gentleness, and selflessness. It teaches that love is not boastful, proud, or self-seeking. Love is not easily angered, keeps no record of wrongs, and rejoices in truth.

Enduring Love: Love is depicted as enduring and persevering. It doesn't waver in the face of challenges or difficulties. It is steadfast and unchanging.

The Impermanence of Knowledge and Prophecy: The chapter contrasts love with the temporary nature of knowledge and prophecy. It suggests that while knowledge and prophecies may fade, love remains eternal.

The Role of Faith and Hope: Love is portrayed as the greatest of virtues, even greater than faith and hope. It is the tie that binds everything together, complementing and enhancing faith and hope.

Maturing Beyond Childhood: The chapter describes the idea that love matures and evolves. It encourages believers to put away childish ways and embrace a deeper, more mature love.

Mirror of God's Love: The chapter reflects God's love for humanity, which is characterized by patience, kindness, and forgiveness. It encourages believers to mirror this divine love in their relationships with others.

Unconditional Love: Love in 1 Corinthians 13 is depicted as unconditional. It is not dependent on the worthiness or actions of the recipient. It extends to all, even to those who might be considered undeserving.

The Call to Practice Love: The passage serves as a call to action. It encourages believers to actively practice love in their interactions with others. Love is not merely a feeling but an intentional choice and a way of life.

Timeless Message: The teachings of 1 Corinthians 13 has a timeless quality. They continue to resonate with people from various backgrounds and faiths. The chapter's lessons about love transcend cultural and religious boundaries.

Incorporating the teachings of 1 Corinthians 13 into one's life can lead to greater compassion, kindness, and a deeper understanding of love. It reminds us that love is not only an emotion but a way of being and relating to others. It encourages a focus on the well-being and welfare of others, even in the face of challenges and conflicts.

Chapter 6
"Love in Action"

Practical application of love in our daily lives, inspired by the Bible.

The practical application of love in our daily lives, as inspired by the Bible, is a foundational aspect of Christian living. The Bible provides numerous guidelines and examples of how love can be applied in our relationships and interactions.

Love for God
- Start each day with prayer and thanksgiving, expressing your love for God and seeking His guidance.
- Dedicate time for Bible study and meditation to deepen your understanding of God's love and His will for your life.
- Worship and attend religious services as acts of love and devotion to God.

Love for Self
- Acknowledge your intrinsic worth as a creation of God and practice self-compassion.
- Care for your physical and mental health, recognizing that your well-being is important.
- Avoid self-criticism and practice self-forgiveness, as God's love extends to you too.

Love for Family
- Prioritize quality time with your family, showing love through communication, support, and presence.
- Resolve conflicts with family members through forgiveness, understanding, and reconciliation.
- Pray for and with your family, seeking God's blessings on your relationships.

Love for Friends
- Cultivate friendships based on trust, mutual support, and respect.
- Be a source of encouragement and comfort to friends in times of need.
- Show gratitude for the gift of friendship and express your love through kind words and actions.

Love for Neighbors

- Extend love to your neighbors by being a good neighbor yourself, helping when needed and fostering a sense of community.
- Practice kindness and hospitality towards those living in your vicinity.
- Engage in acts of service and charity to benefit your community.

Love for Enemies and Difficult People

- Follow Jesus' teachings by praying for and blessing those who may be perceived as enemies or difficult.
- Seek reconciliation and forgiveness, whenever possible, in challenging relationships.
- Show empathy and try to understand the perspective of those with whom you disagree.

Love for Strangers and the Vulnerable:

- Engage in acts of charity and volunteer work to help those in need, following Jesus' example.
- Support initiatives and organizations that assist the vulnerable, such as the poor, the homeless, or refugees.
- Welcome strangers with hospitality and an open heart.

Love in Marriage and Relationships:

- Practice love in marital relationships through communication, mutual respect, and selflessness.
- Prioritize your partner's well-being and growth, nurturing a healthy and loving partnership.
- Seek guidance from the Bible for marital and relationship advice.

Forgiveness and Reconciliation:

- Embrace the biblical principles of forgiveness and reconciliation in relationships.
- Let go of grudges and past wrongs, and actively work towards healing and restoration.
- Follow the model of God's forgiveness as exemplified in the Bible.

Kindness and Generosity:

- Show love through acts of kindness, generosity, and hospitality.
- Be willing to help those in need and share your blessings with others.
- Contribute to charitable causes and organizations that promote love and care for others.

Truth and Honesty:

- Apply love with truth and honesty in your words and actions.

- Communicate openly and transparently, practicing integrity in all your dealings.
- Refrain from deceit or manipulation and encourage honesty in others.

Prayer and Reflection:
- Continuously seek guidance and strength from God through prayer and meditation.
- Reflect on your actions and relationships, asking for God's wisdom in living out His love.
- Make prayer an integral part of your daily life.

Practicing love in our daily lives, as inspired by the Bible, involves intentional efforts to demonstrate love, compassion, and kindness in all our interactions. It's about living out the teachings of the Bible, reflecting God's love in our relationships, and making the world a better place through love and service.

Love can manifest through acts of kindness, compassion, and service to others.

Love can manifest through acts of kindness, compassion, and service to others in various ways, reflecting the core principles of selflessness and care that are emphasized in the Bible. Here's how love can be demonstrated through these actions:

Acts of Kindness:
- **Random Acts of Kindness**: Show love by performing small, unexpected acts of kindness, such as paying for someone's coffee, holding the door open, or leaving an encouraging note.
- Helping in Daily Tasks: Aid those who may need help with daily tasks, whether it's carrying groceries, shoveling snow, or babysitting for a neighbor.
- **Listening Actively**: Practice kindness by being a good listener. Offer your time and attention to those who need someone to talk to.

Compassion:
- **Empathy and Understanding**: Demonstrate love through empathy and understanding. Seek to understand the experiences and emotions of others without judgment.
- **Support in Times of Crisis**: Show compassion by being there for others during difficult times. Offer a shoulder to lean on, a listening ear, or a comforting presence.
- **Advocacy and Social Justice**: Advocate for those who are

marginalized, oppressed, or facing injustice. Compassion can manifest through efforts to address systemic issues and promote equality.

Service to Others:
- Volunteer Work: Engage in volunteer activities that serve the community, such as working at a food bank, serving meals at a homeless shelter, or participating in environmental cleanup.
- Mentorship: Offer guidance and mentorship to individuals seeking support, whether it's in academics, career development, or personal growth.
- Acts of Generosity: Serve others through acts of generosity, such as donating to charitable causes, contributing to fundraisers, or assisting those in financial need.

Caring for the Sick and Vulnerable:
- Visiting the Sick: Show love by visiting the sick in hospitals, nursing homes, or in their own homes. Your presence and good wishes can provide comfort.
- Providing Care and Assistance: Care for the vulnerable by helping the elderly or individuals with disabilities with tasks like shopping, transportation, or personal care.

Fostering Inclusivity:
- Welcoming Strangers: Love can manifest through welcoming strangers and newcomers, helping them acclimate to a new environment and community.
- Building Bridges: Promote inclusivity and unity by connecting with people from diverse backgrounds, fostering understanding, and breaking down barriers.

Teaching and Mentoring:
- Sharing Knowledge: Offer your expertise and knowledge to others, whether through teaching, mentoring, or providing guidance to those seeking to learn and grow.
- Encouraging Growth: Show love by helping individuals reach their potential and achieve their goals. Celebrate their successes and offer support during setbacks.

Reconciliation and Conflict Resolution:
- Seeking Reconciliation: Demonstrate love by initiating reconciliation in strained relationships. Offer forgiveness and work towards healing and restoration.
- Peacemaking: Act as a peacemaker in conflicts between others, helping

them find common ground and resolve disputes.

Prayer and Intercession:
- Prayer for Others: Show love through intercessory prayer, lifting up the needs, concerns, and well-being of others in your prayers.
- Spiritual Support: Offer spiritual support and encouragement to those facing challenges or seeking guidance in their faith journey.

Environmental Stewardship:
-Caring for Creation: Love can manifest through caring for the environment and being a responsible steward of God's creation. Practice sustainable living and participate in conservation efforts.

Acts of Forgiveness:
- Forgiving Others: Show love by extending forgiveness to those who have wronged you. Release grudges and embrace the power of forgiveness for healing and reconciliation.

Acts of kindness, compassion, and service to others are practical expressions of love that align with the teachings of the Bible. They reflect the selfless and caring nature of God's love and provide tangible ways to make a positive impact in the lives of those around you and in your community.

Chapter 7
"Eternal Love"

The promise of eternal love, hope, and redemption found in the Bible.

The promise of eternal love, hope, and redemption found in the Bible is a source of profound comfort and inspiration for many believers. It underlies the core message of salvation and the transformative power of God's love. Here are reflections on these promises:

Eternal Love:
- The Bible teaches that God's love is eternal and unchanging. It is not dependent on our actions or worthiness but is a fundamental aspect of God's character.
- This eternal love provides a sense of security and assurance that, no matter the circumstances, God's love endures. It is a love that transcends time and space.

Hope:
- The Bible is replete with messages of hope. It offers hope to those who are facing trials, suffering, or despair. It assures believers that even in the darkest of times, there is hope for a better future.
- The hope found in the Bible is not wishful thinking but a confident expectation in God's promises. It encourages individuals to trust in God's faithfulness and His plans for their lives.

Redemption:
- The concept of redemption is central to the Christian faith. It signifies the deliverance and transformation of individuals through the atoning work of Jesus Christ.
- The Bible teaches that through faith in Christ, believers can be redeemed from sin, guilt, and the consequences of their actions. This redemption provides a fresh start and a path to reconciliation with God.

Forgiveness:
- The Bible offers the promise of forgiveness, emphasizing that through repentance and faith, individuals can be forgiven for their transgressions.
- This forgiveness is not based on one's merits but is a product of God's grace and love. It leads to the restoration of the relationship between the

individual and God.

Resurrection and Eternal Life:
- The Bible teaches the promise of resurrection and eternal life. Believers are assured that death is not the end but a transition to an eternal existence with God.
- This promise provides comfort in the face of mortality and the loss of loved ones. It affirms the hope of reunion in the presence of God.

Transformation and Renewal:
- The Bible offers the promise of personal transformation and renewal through the power of the Holy Spirit.
- It teaches that believers can experience a change of heart and mind, becoming new creations with the capacity to love, serve, and live in accordance with God's will.

Restoration and Reconciliation:
- The Bible emphasizes the promise of restoration and reconciliation with God and with others. It encourages believers to seek reconciliation and healing in broken relationships.
- This promise inspires efforts to mend what is broken and work towards unity, peace, and justice.

Unconditional Love:
- The Bible teaches that God's love is unconditional, not based on human merit or performance. This love is a source of comfort and acceptance.
- It assures individuals that they are loved by the Creator, flaws and all, and that nothing can separate them from God's love.

In sum, the promise of eternal love, hope, and redemption found in the Bible is a beacon of light and assurance in the lives of many. It signifies the unchanging and compassionate nature of God, offering the hope of a brighter future, forgiveness, transformation, and the assurance of eternal life. These promises serve as a source of strength and inspiration, guiding believers on their spiritual journey and providing solace in times of difficulty and uncertainty.

The ultimate expression of divine love through the crucifixion and resurrection of Jesus.

The crucifixion and resurrection of Jesus are the ultimate expressions of divine love in Christian theology. These events are at the heart of the

Christian faith and carry profound significance as manifestations of God's selfless and sacrificial love. Here's a reflection on the crucifixion and resurrection of Jesus as the pinnacle of divine love:

The Crucifixion - A Sacrificial Act of Love:

- The crucifixion of Jesus is the ultimate act of selfless love. He willingly gave His life as a sacrifice for the sins of humanity.
- This act of crucifixion represents God's deep love for humanity, as it was through the suffering and death of Jesus that redemption and reconciliation with God were made possible.
- Jesus' willingness to endure the agony of the cross demonstrates a love that is willing to bear the consequences of human sin and brokenness.

Atonement and Redemption:

- The crucifixion is central to the concept of atonement, as it is believed to be the means through which the sins of humanity were forgiven.
- Jesus' sacrifice on the cross is seen as the perfect and sufficient payment for human sin, allowing believers to be reconciled with God and experience forgiveness and salvation.

Identification with Human Suffering:

- In His crucifixion, Jesus identified with human suffering. He experienced physical pain, rejection, and isolation, making Him a compassionate High Priest who can empathize with the struggles of humanity.
- This identification with suffering is a powerful expression of love, as it shows that God understands and shares in the hardships of human existence.

The Resurrection - A Triumph of Love:

- The resurrection of Jesus is the triumph of divine love over death and sin. It demonstrates God's power over all forces of darkness.
- The resurrection is a source of hope and assurance, as it signifies that death is not the end. Believers can have confidence in the promise of eternal life.

Eternal Life and New Creation:

- The resurrection points to the promise of eternal life for believers. It assures them that, through faith in Jesus, they can have a share in God's new creation.
- This new creation is characterized by love, justice, and the absence of suffering, making it the ultimate expression of divine love for humanity.

A Model for Selflessness:
- The crucifixion and resurrection of Jesus serve as a model for selflessness and sacrificial love. It encourages believers to love and serve others as Jesus did.
- This model calls individuals to extend their love beyond themselves and to be willing to make sacrifices for the well-being of others.

In summary, the crucifixion and resurrection of Jesus stand as the ultimate expression of divine love in the Christian faith. They represent God's sacrificial love for humanity, the means of redemption and reconciliation, and the triumph over sin and death. These events continue to inspire believers to live lives characterized by selfless love, compassion, and hope, reflecting the transformative power of God's love in the world.

Chapter 8
Living out Love in Community

Living out the message of divine love in our communities is essential for embodying the teachings of the Bible. The essence of love is not solitary but thrives within the fabric of relationships. This chapter delves into the intricate dynamics of fostering love within families, churches, and broader communities, recognizing that our interconnectedness deepens our understanding and experience of divine love.

Within the family unit, love serves as the foundation for healthy relationships. Whether between spouses, parents and children, or siblings, love manifests in various forms: care, sacrifice, patience, and understanding. The Bible presents numerous examples of familial love, such as the unconditional love of the prodigal son's father or the sacrificial love of Ruth for Naomi. These narratives teach us that love within the family is not contingent on perfection but on a commitment to support, nurture, and forgive one another.

Similarly, within the church community, love is the binding force that unites believers in Christ. The early Christian communities, as described in the New Testament, exemplified this love through their mutual care, generosity, and devotion to one another. Acts 2:42-47 portrays a community where believers shared their possessions, worshipped together, and supported each other spiritually and materially. This spirit of love within the church serves as a model for contemporary Christian communities, urging them to prioritize unity, humility, and service.

Beyond the confines of familial and church relationships, divine love calls us to extend our love to the broader community. This includes our neighbors, colleagues, and even strangers. The parable of the Good Samaritan illustrates the radical nature of love, transcending societal divisions and prejudices to care for those in need. In a world marked by division and discord, the call to love our neighbors challenges us to break down barriers, build bridges, and cultivate a culture of empathy, compassion, and solidarity.

Practical strategies for fostering love within communities include creating spaces for open communication and mutual support, organizing community service projects, and promoting inclusivity and diversity. By prioritizing relationships and investing in the well-being of others, communities can become vibrant expressions of divine love, where individuals feel valued, supported, and empowered to thrive.

Chapter 9
Overcoming Challenges with Love

When confronted with challenges, whether personal or societal, the transformative power of divine love becomes apparent. This chapter delves into the ways in which love empowers us to overcome adversity, confront injustice, and navigate the complexities of life with courage and grace.

At the heart of divine love lies a profound sense of comfort and solace in times of trial. The psalmist's declaration in Psalm 34:18 reassures us of God's close presence and saving grace for the brokenhearted and downtrodden. This assurance not only provides a sense of companionship but also infuses us with the strength needed to weather life's storms. Knowing that we are unconditionally loved by a higher power enables us to find resilience even in the darkest of times.

Furthermore, love serves as a catalyst for social change, inspiring us to confront the injustices and inequities that pervade our world. Rooted in the prophetic tradition of the Bible, love compels us to speak out against oppression, advocate for the marginalized, and strive for a more just and equitable society. The example of Jesus Christ, who tirelessly championed the cause of the poor, the marginalized, and the oppressed, serves as a beacon guiding us toward social justice and transformation.

In practical terms, overcoming challenges with love requires us to cultivate resilience, empathy, and compassion. This entails acknowledging and confronting our own biases and prejudices, listening with humility to the experiences of others, and standing in solidarity with those who are suffering. By embracing love as a guiding principle in our lives, we can transform adversity into opportunities for growth, healing, and reconciliation.

Cultivating resilience involves developing a mindset that sees challenges as opportunities for personal growth and development. Rather than viewing setbacks as insurmountable obstacles, we can approach them with a sense of optimism and determination, trusting in the power of love to see us through. Resilience also entails seeking support from others, whether through close relationships, faith communities, or professional counseling, recognizing that we do not have to face our challenges alone.

Empathy and compassion are essential components of overcoming challenges with love. By putting ourselves in the shoes of others and seeking to understand their perspectives, we can forge deeper connections and foster a sense of solidarity. This requires us to listen actively and attentively to the experiences of those who are different from us, acknowledging their pain and struggles with empathy and compassion.

Standing in solidarity with those who are suffering involves actively advocating for their rights and well-being. This may take the form of participating in protests and demonstrations, signing petitions, or supporting organizations that work to address systemic injustices. By leveraging our privilege and resources to uplift those who are marginalized and oppressed, we can help create a more just and equitable society for all.

In conclusion, overcoming challenges with love is both a personal and collective endeavor. By cultivating resilience, empathy, and compassion, we can confront adversity with courage and grace, drawing strength from the transformative power of divine love. As we strive to create a more just and compassionate world, may we be guided by the timeless wisdom of love, knowing that it has the power to heal, reconcile, and transform.

Chapter 10
Extending Love Beyond Borders

The message of divine love transcends cultural, social, and geographical boundaries, calling us to embrace the diversity of God's creation and to extend love to all people, regardless of their background or circumstances. This chapter explores the universal nature of love and its transformative power to bridge divides, foster understanding, and promote justice and equality on a global scale.

At its core, divine love is inclusive and expansive, encompassing people of every nation, tribe, and tongue. The Apostle Paul declares, "There is neither Jew nor Greek, there is neither slave nor free, there is no male and female, for you are all one in Christ Jesus" (Galatians 3:28). This vision of unity in diversity challenges us to break down the barriers of prejudice and discrimination that divide us and to embrace the richness of human... ... diversity as a reflection of God's love for all of creation.

The universal nature of divine love compels us to extend our love beyond borders, reaching out to people of different cultures, backgrounds, and circumstances. This requires us to move beyond our comfort zones and engage with those who may be different from us, recognizing the inherent dignity and worth of every individual.

One of the key aspects of extending love beyond borders is fostering understanding and empathy across cultural divides. This involves taking the time to listen to and learn from people whose experiences and perspectives may differ from our own. By engaging in meaningful dialogue and building relationships based on mutual respect and trust, we can break down stereotypes and misconceptions, paving the way for greater understanding and cooperation.

Moreover, extending love beyond borders requires us to confront the systemic injustices and inequalities that perpetuate division and exclusion. This may involve advocating for policies and practices that promote equality and justice for all people, regardless of their race, ethnicity, or socioeconomic status. It may also involve supporting organizations and initiatives that work to address issues such as poverty, discrimination, and human rights abuses on a global scale.

Practical ways to extend love beyond borders include participating in cross-cultural exchange programs, volunteering with international aid organizations, and supporting fair trade initiatives that promote economic justice and empowerment for marginalized communities. By actively engaging with the world beyond our own borders, we can broaden our perspective, deepen our empathy, and contribute to the creation of a more just and compassionate global community.

Ultimately, extending love beyond borders reflects our commitment to embodying the values of love, justice, and equality that lie at the heart of the gospel message. It is an acknowledgment of our shared humanity and interconnectedness, and a recognition of the inherent dignity and worth of every individual. As we strive to extend love beyond borders, may we be guided by the spirit of compassion and solidarity, working together to create a world where all people are valued, respected, and embraced.

Chapter 11
Nurturing Love in the Next Generation

As stewards of divine love, we are called to nurture the values of love, kindness, and compassion in the next generation. This chapter explores the role of parents, educators, and mentors in instilling these virtues in children and young people, equipping them to become agents of love and transformation in their communities and beyond.

Parents play a crucial role in shaping the character and values of their children. The Bible emphasizes the importance of teaching children about the love of God and modeling love in our interactions with them. Deuteronomy 6:6-7 instructs parents to "impress these commandments on your children. Talk about them when you sit at home and when you walk along the road, when you lie down and when you get up." This holistic approach to education emphasizes the integration of faith and daily life, creating a seamless environment where children can observe, learn, and internalize the principles of love and compassion.

Modeling love begins with how parents treat each other and interact with their children. Children learn by example, observing the way their parents communicate, resolve conflicts, and express affection. When parents demonstrate love, kindness, and empathy towards one another and towards their children, they provide a powerful template for healthy relationships and positive behavior.

In addition to modeling love, parents can actively teach and reinforce the values of love and compassion through intentional conversations and activities. This includes reading and discussing stories from the Bible that illustrate love in action, such as the parable of the Good Samaritan or Jesus' teachings on forgiveness and mercy. Parents can also engage their children in acts of service and kindness, such as volunteering together at a local shelter or participating in a community cleanup project. These experiences help children develop empathy and compassion for others and cultivate a heart for service.

Beyond the home, educators and mentors play a significant role in nurturing love and compassion in young people. Teachers have the opportunity to create classroom environments that foster empathy, respect, and inclusivity. By incorporating lessons on kindness, empathy, and diversity into the curriculum, educators can help students develop a deeper understanding of the importance of love and compassion in their interactions with others.

Mentors, whether within the church or community, provide additional support and guidance to young people as they navigate the challenges of adolescence and young adulthood. Mentoring relationships offers a safe space for young people to explore their faith, ask questions, and receive encouragement and wisdom from someone who has walked the path before them. Mentors can model love and compassion in their interactions with their mentees and provide guidance on how to live out these values in their daily lives.

Overall, nurturing love in the next generation requires a holistic approach that encompasses modeling, teaching, and mentoring. By instilling the values of love, kindness, and compassion in children and young people, parents, educators, and mentors can empower them to become agents of love and transformation in their communities and beyond. As we invest in the next generation, we lay the foundation for a future filled with compassion, empathy, and justice.

Chapter 12
Love in Action: Social Justice and Advocacy

Divine love compels us to advocate for social justice and equality, confronting systemic injustices and working towards a world where all people are treated with dignity and respect. This chapter explores how love motivates us to engage in activism and advocacy, challenging oppressive structures and striving to create a more just and equitable society for all.

The Bible is replete with calls for justice and compassion for the marginalized and oppressed. Micah 6:8 exhorts us to "act justly, love mercy, and walk humbly with your God." This mandate to pursue justice and mercy is central to the message of the prophets and the teachings of Jesus Christ, who identified with the poor, the marginalized, and the oppressed and called his followers to do the same.

Practical strategies for social justice and advocacy include raising awareness about... ... systemic injustices, advocating for policy changes, and actively working to dismantle oppressive structures in society. Love in action requires us to not only feel compassion for those who are marginalized and oppressed but to actively work towards creating a more just and equitable world for them.

Raising awareness about systemic injustices is an important first step in social justice advocacy. This involves educating ourselves and others about the root causes of injustice, whether it be racism, sexism, economic inequality, or other forms of discrimination. By shining a light on these issues and bringing them into public discourse, we can mobilize support for change and challenge the status quo.

Advocating for policy changes is another crucial aspect of social justice activism. This may involve lobbying elected officials, organizing grassroots campaigns, or participating in protests and demonstrations to demand legislative reforms that address systemic injustices. By leveraging our collective voice and power, we can pressure policymakers to enact laws and policies that promote equality, justice, and human rights for all.

Additionally, social justice advocacy requires us to actively work to dismantle oppressive structures in society. This may involve challenging institutionalized forms of discrimination and bias within systems such as education, healthcare, criminal justice, and employment. It may also involve supporting grassroots initiatives and community-led efforts to empower marginalized communities and address their unique needs and concerns.

Practicing love in action means standing in solidarity with those who are marginalized and oppressed, amplifying their voices, and advocating for their rights and dignity. It means recognizing our own privilege and using it to uplift others, rather than perpetuating systems of oppression. It means actively working to create a world where all people are treated with dignity, respect, and compassion, regardless of their race, ethnicity, gender, sexual orientation, or socioeconomic status.

In conclusion, love in action is a powerful force for social change, motivating us to confront injustice and inequality and to work towards a more just and equitable world for all. By embodying the values of love, justice, and compassion in our words and actions, we can make a meaningful difference in the lives of those who are marginalized and oppressed and contribute to the creation of a more just and compassionate society for generations to come.

Chapter 13
Sustaining Love in Times of Trial

Divine love sustains us during times of trial and adversity, offering comfort, hope, and strength to persevere through life's challenges. This chapter explores how love provides a steadfast anchor amidst life's storms, enabling us to find solace and resilience even in the most trying of circumstances.

In times of trial and adversity, the sustaining power of divine love becomes abundantly clear. Unlike fleeting emotions or temporary fixes, divine love offers a profound and enduring source of comfort, hope, and strength. It is a love that transcends human understanding, providing us with a sense of peace and assurance even when the world around us seems to be falling apart.

One of the ways in which love sustains us during times of trial is by offering us a sense of companionship and solidarity. The psalmist reminds us that "even though I walk through the darkest valley, I will fear no evil, for you are with me" (Psalm 23:4). In moments of despair and loneliness, knowing that we are not alone but are held in the loving embrace of a higher power can provide us with the courage and strength to keep moving forward.

Moreover, love sustains us by instilling within us a sense of hope and optimism for the future. The Apostle Paul writes, "And now these three remain: faith, hope, and love. But the greatest of these is love" (1 Corinthians 13:13). Even in the midst of life's darkest moments, love reminds us that there is always hope for a better tomorrow. It gives us the resilience to persevere through hardship and adversity, knowing that brighter days are ahead.

Love also sustains us by empowering us to find meaning and purpose in our suffering. Rather than viewing trials as meaningless or random occurrences, love helps us to see them as opportunities for growth, transformation, and redemption. The Apostle James encourages us to "consider it pure joy, my brothers and sisters, whenever you face trials of many kinds, because you know that the testing of your faith produces perseverance" (James 1:2-3). Through love, we can find purpose in our pain and emerge from our trials stronger, wiser, and more compassionate than before.

Practical strategies for sustaining love in times of trial include drawing strength from spiritual practices such as prayer, meditation, and scripture reading, seeking support from loved ones and faith communities, and engaging in acts of self-care and self-compassion. By nurturing our relationship with the divine and surrounding ourselves with a supportive community of fellow believers, we can tap into the sustaining power of love and find the strength and resilience to persevere through life's challenges.

In conclusion, sustaining love in times of trial is a testament to the enduring power of divine love to provide us with comfort, hope, and strength even in the darkest of times. By anchoring ourselves in the love of God and drawing strength from our faith and community, we can weather life's storms with grace and resilience, knowing that we are held in the loving embrace of a higher power that will never let us go.

Chapter 14
Love's Eternal Promise

In this concluding chapter, we reflect on the eternal promise of divine love as revealed in the Bible. Love is not just a temporary emotion or fleeting feeling but an enduring reality that transcends time and space. The Bible assures us that nothing can separate us from the love of God (Romans 8:38-39), and that love will ultimately triumph over sin and death.

The promise of divine love gives us hope for the future and confidence in the goodness and faithfulness of God. As we journey through life, facing its joys and sorrows, its triumphs and tribulations, we can take comfort in the knowledge that we are held secure in the love of our Creator. This love gives us the courage to face the unknown, the strength to persevere through adversity, and the assurance of eternal life with God.

In conclusion, "Divine Love: Exploring the Heart of the Bible" invites us to make love the cornerstone of our faith and our lives. Through embodying the principles of divine love, we can experience its transformative power in our lives and in the world around us.

The eternal promise of divine love is a central theme throughout the Bible, from Genesis to Revelation. It is a promise that speaks to the unchanging nature of God's love and its capacity to transcend the limitations of human understanding. As the Apostle Paul writes in Romans 8:38-39, "For I am convinced that neither death nor life, neither angels nor demons, neither the present nor the future, nor any powers, neither height nor depth, nor anything else in all creation, will be able to separate us from the love of God that is in Christ Jesus our Lord."

This promise of unfailing love gives us hope and assurance in the midst of life's uncertainties. It reminds us that no matter what challenges or trials we may face, we are never alone, for God's love is with us always. It is a love that sustains us through the darkest of times, giving us the strength and courage to persevere.

Moreover, the promise of divine love extends beyond this life into eternity. It is a love that conquers sin and death, offering us the hope of resurrection and eternal life with God. As Jesus himself declares in John 3:16, "For God so loved the world that he gave his one and only Son, that whoever believes in him shall not perish but have eternal life." This promise of eternal life with God is the ultimate expression of divine love, offering us the assurance of a future filled with joy, peace, and fulfillment in the presence of our Creator.

In conclusion, "Divine Love: Exploring the Heart of the Bible" reminds us of the profound and transformative power of divine love in our lives. It calls us to make love the cornerstone of our faith and our lives, embracing its eternal promise and allowing it to guide and shape us in all that we do. As we journey through life, may we be inspired by the enduring love of God and seek to share that love with others, bringing hope, healing, and reconciliation to a world in need.

Chapter 15
Love's Transformative Impact on Relationships

Love's transformative impact extends beyond individual lives; it profoundly influences our relationships with others. This chapter explores how divine love reshapes our interactions, fostering deeper connections, empathy, and understanding. Whether in friendships, familial bonds, or romantic relationships, love transforms how we perceive and relate to one another. Through forgiveness, reconciliation, and mutual respect, love has the power to heal wounds, mend broken relationships, and cultivate enduring bonds built on trust and compassion.

Love has an extraordinary capacity to transform the dynamics of our relationships, permeating them with understanding, empathy, and profound connection. This chapter delves into the ways in which divine love reshapes our interactions, nurturing deeper bonds and fostering growth within friendships, familial relationships, and romantic partnerships.

At the heart of love's transformative impact on relationships lies the principle of forgiveness. Love teaches us to release resentment and let go of grudges, allowing us to move forward with compassion and understanding. Through forgiveness, we open the door to reconciliation, healing the wounds of the past and restoring harmony to our relationships. Whether it's forgiving a friend for a misunderstanding, reconciling with a family member after a disagreement, or extending grace to a partner in a romantic relationship, love enables us to transcend hurt and conflict, paving the way for greater intimacy and connection.

Furthermore, love cultivates empathy, enabling us to see the world through the eyes of others and understand their experiences and perspectives more deeply. By empathizing with our loved ones, we create space for vulnerability and authenticity within our relationships, fostering a sense of mutual understanding and support. This empathetic connection strengthens the bonds between us, allowing us to navigate life's challenges together with grace and compassion.

Mutual respect is another cornerstone of love's transformative impact on relationships. Love teaches us to honor the inherent dignity and worth of every individual, valuing their unique contributions and perspectives. When we approach our relationships with respect and appreciation, we create an environment of trust and mutual admiration, where each person feels valued, seen, and heard. This foundation of respect forms the bedrock of healthy, fulfilling relationships, allowing us to build enduring bonds of trust and companionship.

In romantic relationships, love deepens our emotional intimacy and strengthens our commitment to one another. Love teaches us to prioritize the well-being and happiness of our partners, nurturing a relationship based on mutual respect, trust, and shared values. Through acts of kindness, generosity, and selflessness, we express our love and devotion, creating a partnership characterized by warmth, affection, and companionship.

In conclusion, love's transformative impact on relationships is profound and far-reaching. By cultivating forgiveness, empathy, and mutual respect, we create a foundation of trust and understanding that sustains and nourishes our connections with others. Whether in friendships, familial bonds, or romantic relationships, love has the power to heal, strengthen, and transform, enriching our lives with profound meaning and fulfillment. As we embrace the principles of divine love in our relationships, we unlock the full potential of human connection, creating a world where love reigns supreme.

Chapter 16
Love's Role in Personal Growth and Fulfillment

Love's role in personal growth and fulfillment is profound, serving as a guiding light on the journey of self-discovery and inner transformation. This chapter explores how embracing divine love empowers us to embark on a path of self-realization, acceptance, and fulfillment.

At its core, love invites us to recognize and embrace our inherent worth and value as individuals. Through the lens of divine love, we come to understand that our worthiness is not contingent upon external achievements or validation from others but is rooted in our intrinsic nature as beloved creations of the Divine. This realization frees us from the shackles of self-doubt and insecurity, empowering us to embrace our true selves with confidence and authenticity.

Love encourages us to cultivate a deep sense of self-compassion and acceptance, embracing all aspects of ourselves, including our flaws and imperfections. Rather than striving for unattainable perfection, love teaches us to embrace our humanity with kindness and understanding, recognizing that our vulnerabilities are an essential part of what makes us whole. Through self-compassion practices such as mindfulness, meditation, and journaling, we learn to extend grace to ourselves and cultivate a greater sense of inner peace and fulfillment.

Furthermore, love inspires us to pursue our passions and cultivate our talents, unleashing our creative potential and igniting a sense of purpose and meaning in our lives. When we align our actions with our deepest desires and values, we experience a profound sense of fulfillment and joy, knowing that we are living in alignment with our true selves. Whether it's pursuing a creative endeavor, embarking on a new career path, or dedicating ourselves to a cause we believe in, love empowers us to follow our hearts and pursue our dreams with courage and conviction.

Self-love and self-care practices are essential components of embracing love's role in personal growth and fulfillment. By prioritizing our well-being and nurturing our physical, emotional, and spiritual health, we create a solid foundation for growth and self-discovery. This may involve setting boundaries, practicing self-care rituals, seeking support from loved ones, and engaging in activities that bring us joy and rejuvenation. Through self-love and self-care, we replenish our energy reserves, cultivate resilience, and unlock our full potential for growth and fulfillment.

In conclusion, love's role in personal growth and fulfillment is transformative and empowering. By embracing divine love and cultivating self-compassion, acceptance, and authenticity, we embark on a journey of self-discovery and inner transformation. Through self-love and self-care practices, we nurture our well-being and unlock our potential, embracing a life of purpose, joy, and fulfillment. As we embrace love as the guiding force in our lives, we open ourselves to a world of infinite possibilities, where our true selves can flourish and thrive.

Chapter 17
Love's Impact on Mental Health and Well-being

Love's impact on mental health and well-being is indeed profound, offering solace, support, and a sense of belonging to the mind, body, and spirit. This chapter delves into the transformative power of divine love as a source of healing and restoration, promoting resilience, emotional stability, and overall well-being.

At its core, divine love offers unconditional acceptance and support, serving as a beacon of hope and comfort in times of stress or anxiety. When we feel loved and valued, we experience a sense of security and reassurance that strengthens our resilience in the face of life's challenges. Love provides a safe harbor for our emotions, allowing us to express ourselves authentically and seek support when needed, without fear of judgment or rejection.

Moreover, acts of kindness, compassion, and altruism associated with love have been shown to have a positive impact on mental health and well-being. When we engage in acts of love and kindness towards others, whether through volunteering, helping a friend in need, or simply offering a listening ear, we experience a sense of fulfillment and connection that boosts our mood and reduces feelings of loneliness and isolation. These acts of love not only benefit the recipient but also nourish our own well-being, fostering a sense of purpose, belonging, and satisfaction in our lives.

Love also promotes positive emotions such as joy, gratitude, and contentment, which have been linked to improved mental health and well-being. When we cultivate a mindset of love and gratitude, we shift our focus away from negative thoughts and emotions towards the abundance and beauty that surround us. This shift in perspective helps us to cope more effectively with stress and adversity, fostering emotional resilience and psychological well-being.

Furthermore, love fosters a sense of belonging and connection, which are essential elements of mental health and well-being. When we feel loved and connected to others, we experience a sense of belongingness that buffers against feelings of loneliness and isolation. Love strengthens our social bonds and fosters a sense of community, providing us with a support network of friends, family, and loved ones who uplift and encourage us during times of need.

In conclusion, love's impact on mental health and well-being is profound and far-reaching. By prioritizing love in our lives and nurturing our relationships with others, we cultivate emotional resilience, promote positive emotions, and foster a sense of belonging and connection that contributes to overall mental health and well-being. As we embrace the transformative power of divine love, we unlock the full potential of our minds, bodies, and spirits, experiencing greater peace, joy, and fulfillment in our lives.

Chapter 18
Love's Influence on Leadership and Service

Love's influence on leadership and service is profound, shaping how we engage with others and effect positive change in our communities. This chapter explores the principles of servant leadership, rooted in love, humility, and empathy, and how leaders who lead with love prioritize the well-being and development of those they serve.

Servant leadership, guided by love, is characterized by a deep commitment to serving others and empowering them to reach their full potential. Rather than seeking power or control, servant leaders approach leadership with humility and compassion, recognizing that their primary role is to support and uplift those they lead. Love serves as the foundation of their leadership philosophy, inspiring them to cultivate a culture of collaboration, trust, and empowerment within their organizations or communities.

One of the key principles of servant leadership is prioritizing the well-being and development of those they serve. Love compels leaders to put the needs of others before their own, seeking to nurture their growth and success. By fostering a supportive and inclusive environment, servant leaders create space for individuals to thrive, unlocking their potential and enabling them to make meaningful contributions to the organization or community.

Furthermore, love fuels acts of service and philanthropy, empowering individuals to address social issues and uplift marginalized communities. Servant leaders recognize their responsibility to use their influence and resources for the greater good, leveraging their platform to advocate for justice, equality, and human rights. Whether through volunteering, advocacy, or philanthropy, leaders who lead with love seek to create a more just and equitable society where all individuals have the opportunity to flourish.

Love also fosters a culture of collaboration and teamwork, where individuals feel valued, respected, and empowered to contribute their unique talents and perspectives. Servant leaders prioritize open communication, active listening, and empathy, creating a space where diverse voices are heard and respected. By building strong relationships based on trust and mutual respect, servant leaders create a foundation for collective action and positive change.

In conclusion, love's influence on leadership and service is transformative, empowering individuals to lead with compassion, humility, and empathy. Servant leaders who prioritize love seek to uplift and empower those they serve, fostering a culture of collaboration, trust, and empowerment within their organizations or communities. Through acts of service and philanthropy, they harness the power of love to address social issues, uplift marginalized communities, and create a more just and equitable society for all.

Chapter 19
Love's Connection to Spiritual Growth and Enlightenment

Love's connection to spiritual growth and enlightenment is profound, offering a pathway to greater intimacy with the Divine and a deeper understanding of the sacred mysteries of life. This chapter explores how embracing divine love enriches our spiritual journey, leading to a heightened sense of awareness, consciousness, and spiritual fulfillment.

At its essence, love is the language of the Divine, the universal force that connects us to the source of all creation. When we embrace divine love, we open our hearts to the presence of God within and around us, experiencing a profound sense of connection and communion with the sacred. Love serves as a bridge between the material and the spiritual realms, guiding us on a journey of self-discovery and transformation.

Practices such as prayer, meditation, and contemplation are essential tools for cultivating a deeper relationship with God and experiencing moments of spiritual enlightenment. Through prayer, we communicate with the Divine, expressing our gratitude, seeking guidance, and surrendering our will to the higher power. Meditation allows us to quiet the mind, still the ego, and open ourselves to the presence of God, experiencing moments of profound clarity, insight, and revelation. Contemplation invites us to reflect on the mysteries of life, pondering the nature of existence, the purpose of suffering, and the ultimate meaning of our lives.

Love's connection to spiritual growth and enlightenment is not limited to solitary practices; it also extends to our relationships with others and our engagement with the world. When we approach life with love and compassion, we recognize the inherent divinity within each person and honor the sacredness of all creation. Love inspires us to act with kindness, generosity, and empathy, cultivating a spirit of unity and harmony in our interactions with others.

Moreover, love opens our hearts to the interconnectedness of all life, fostering a sense of reverence and awe for the beauty and diversity of creation. As we deepen our understanding of love's connection to spiritual growth and enlightenment, we recognize that we are all interconnected and interdependent, part of a larger tapestry of existence that transcends time and space.

In conclusion, love's connection to spiritual growth and enlightenment is profound and transformative. By embracing divine love and engaging in practices that cultivate a deeper relationship with God, we open ourselves to moments of profound insight, revelation, and spiritual fulfillment. Love serves as a guiding light on our spiritual journey, leading us to greater awareness, consciousness, and unity with the Divine. As we deepen our understanding of love's role in our lives, we unlock the full potential of our spiritual journey, experiencing greater peace, joy, and fulfillment in our connection to God and all of creation.

Chapter 20
Love's Legacy: Passing on the Torch.

Love's legacy is one of the most precious gifts we can pass on to future generations. As we conclude our exploration of divine love, we reflect on its enduring impact and our responsibility to ensure that its light continues to shine brightly in the world. This chapter examines how our commitment to love shapes the world we leave behind and influences the lives of those who come after us.

At its core, love is a timeless and universal force that transcends boundaries of time and space. By embodying the principles of divine love in our words and actions, we leave a lasting imprint on the hearts and minds of others, inspiring them to carry forward the message of love and continue the journey of transformation and redemption.

Intentional acts of kindness, compassion, and service are the hallmarks of love's legacy. Whether it's volunteering in our communities, lending a helping hand to those in need, or simply offering a listening ear to a friend in distress, each act of love contributes to the collective well-being of humanity. These small acts of kindness have the power to ripple outward, creating a wave of love and positivity that touches the lives of countless individuals, both now and in the future.

Moreover, love's legacy is reflected in the way we nurture and mentor the next generation. By modeling love, empathy, and compassion in our relationships with children and young people, we instill within them the values of kindness, generosity, and empathy. We empower them to become agents of positive change in their communities, carrying forward the torch of love and continuing the work of building a more just and compassionate world.

As stewards of divine love, we entrust the future to the hands of those who will follow, confident in the power of love to guide them on their path. We cultivate a legacy of love that transcends time and space, leaving an indelible mark on the world that will endure for generations to come. In doing so, we honor the timeless truth that love is the greatest legacy we can leave behind, a legacy that has the power to transform hearts, heal wounds, and illuminate the path to a brighter future for all.

Conclusion:

"Divine Love: Exploring the Heart of the Bible" beautifully encapsulates the central theme of love in the Bible and its transformative power. Love is not just a concept or an abstract idea; it is the very essence of the Bible's message. This exploration has reminded us of that love, as depicted in the Bible, is an active and powerful force that can bring about positive change in our lives and in the world.

As we immerse ourselves in the Bible's teachings on love, we are called to embrace this love in our own lives. We are encouraged to embody it through acts of kindness, compassion, and service to others. The Bible's message of love is not confined to the pages of a book but is meant to be lived out in our daily interactions with family, friends, neighbors, and even those who may be considered difficult or challenging.

Moreover, the concept of divine love in the Bible reveals a love that is unconditional, selfless, and redemptive. It offers hope, forgiveness, and the promise of eternal life. It is a love that has the power to heal, reconcile, and transform. This love is not limited to a select few but is available to all who seek it.

In conclusion, "Divine Love: Exploring the Heart of the Bible" inspires us to make love the cornerstone of our faith and our lives. It reminds us that love is not just a theme in the Bible; it is the heart of the Bible. By embracing and sharing this divine love, we can contribute to a world that is filled with compassion, hope, and redemption. Love, as revealed in the Bible, is a force that can bring about lasting change and make the world a better place.

www.ingramcontent.com/pod-product-compliance
Lightning Source LLC
LaVergne TN
LVHW010506160826
845677LV00012B/2679

* 9 7 9 8 8 8 2 1 8 4 4 8 2 *